SOUTH AMERICA

by Claire Vanden Branden

Cody Koala
An Imprint of Pop!
popbooksonline.com

abdobooks.com
Published by Pop!, a division of ABDO, PO Box 398166, Minneapolis, Minnesota 55439.

Printed in the United States of America, North Mankato, Minnesota

092018
012019

THIS BOOK CONTAINS RECYCLED MATERIALS

Cover Photo: Shutterstock Images
Interior Photos: Shutterstock Images, 1, 5 (bottom left), 5 (bottom right), 9, 11, 13, 14; Andre Penner/AP Images, 5 (top); Red Line Editorial, 6; iStockphoto, 10; Renato Chalu/AP Images, 15; Fernando Vergara/AP Images, 19 (top); Rodrigo Abd/AP Images, 19 (bottom left); Felipe Dana/AP Images, 19 (bottom right); Martin Mejia/AP Images, 20

Editor: Charly Haley
Series Designer: Laura Mitchell

Library of Congress Control Number: 2018949682

Publisher's Cataloging-in-Publication Data
Names: Vanden Branden, Claire, author.
Title: South America / by Claire Vanden Branden.
Description: Minneapolis, Minnesota: Pop!, 2019 | Series: Continents | Includes online resources and index.
Identifiers: ISBN 9781532161759 (lib. bdg.) | ISBN 9781641855464 (pbk) | ISBN 9781532162817 (ebook)
Subjects: LCSH: South America--Juvenile literature. | Continents--Juvenile literature. | Geography--Juvenile literature.
Classification: DDC 918--dc23

Hello! My name is

Cody Koala

Pop open this book and you'll find QR codes like this one, loaded with information, so you can learn even more!

Scan this code* and others like it while you read, or visit the website below to make this book pop.

popbooksonline.com/south-america

*Scanning QR codes requires a web-enabled smart device with a QR code reader app and a camera.

Table of Contents

Chapter 1

South America

South America has 12 countries. The **continent** touches the Pacific Ocean and the Atlantic Ocean.

Watch a video here!

GULF OF MEXICO
ATLANTIC OCEAN
CARIBBEAN SEA
GUYANA
CENTRAL AMERICA
VENEZUELA
SURINAME
FRENCH GUIANA
ECUADOR
COLOMBIA
AMAZON RAIN FOREST
AMAZON RIVER
PERU
ANDES MOUNTAINS
BOLIVIA
BRAZIL
ATACAMA DESERT
PACIFIC OCEAN
PARAGUAY
CHILE
ARGENTINA
URUGUAY
MAP OF SOUTH AMERICA

South America is connected to North America. Between them is a section of land called Central America.

Brazil is the biggest country in South America. It also has the most people.

Chapter 2

Weather and Land

South America has very hot places near the **equator**. There are warm beaches and **rain forests**. But there are also some cold places in South America.

Learn more here!

The Andes Mountains are in South America. This is the longest **mountain range** in the world.

South America also has the world's driest desert. The Atacama Desert in Chile gets less than one inch of rain per year!

Chapter 3

Animals and Plants

The Amazon rain forest is in South America. It is the world's largest jungle. There are more kinds of plants and animals there than anywhere else in the world.

toucan

Complete an activity here!

sloth

Sloths are one animal in the Amazon. Toucans and parrots live there too. South America also has many lizards and frogs.

More than 2 million kinds of bugs live in the Amazon!

But the Amazon is being destroyed. People are cutting down the trees to build cities and farms. This hurts the plants and animals. Scientists are trying to help.

OMA
MRV
10

Chapter 4

People of South America

South America is home to more than 400 million people. Many people who live there speak Spanish. People in Brazil speak Portuguese.

Learn more here!

There are many groups of people in South America. The Incas are the continent's most well-known **Indigenous People**. People from around the world visit **ancient** Inca cities today.

Millions of people speak Indigenous languages in South America.

Making Connections

Text-to-Self

The Amazon rain forest has many different plants and animals. Would you like to see any of these in real life? Which ones would you like to see?

Text-to-Text

Have you read another book about South America? What did you learn?

Text-to-World

The Amazon rain forest is being destroyed. Why do you think that it is important for scientists to help stop people from cutting down the trees?

Glossary

ancient – from a long time ago.

continent – one of the seven large landmasses on Earth.

equator – an imaginary line that divides Earth in half equally.

Indigenous People – the first group of people in an area.

mountain range – a line of mountains connected together.

rain forest – a tropical forest with many different plants and heavy rainfall.

Index

Online Resources

popbooksonline.com

Thanks for reading this Cody Koala book!

Scan this code* and others like it in this book, or visit the website below to make this book pop!

popbooksonline.com/south-america

*Scanning QR codes requires a web-enabled smart device with a QR code reader app and a camera.